"THE BLESSING OF TH[E LORD MAKES RICH AND ADDS]
NO SORROW."

WHAT I'VE LEARNED ABOUT
THE BLESSING

BIBLICAL KEYS FOR FINANCIAL INCREASE

TED SHUTTLESWORTH

Unless otherwise indicated, all Scripture quotations are from the King James Version of the Bible.

What I've Learned About THE BLESSING
ISBN 978-0-9820619-1-6

Copyright © 2012 by Ted Shuttlesworth

All rights reserved. Content and/or cover may not be reproduced in whole or in part or in any form without the express written consent of the publisher.

www.tedshuttlesworth.com

Published by T.S.E.A., Inc.
Post Office Box 7
Farmington, West Virginia 26571
USA

Cover design by Ted Shuttlesworth Jr.

Printed in the United States of America

TABLE OF CONTENTS

CHAPTER ONE — 5
    GOD WORKS FROM THE INSIDE OUT

CHAPTER TWO — 10
    GOD'S KEY TO MULTIPLYING MONEY

CHAPTER THREE — 15
    SEND NOW PROSPERITY!

CHAPTER FOUR — 20
    THE BLESSING IS ALREADY IN YOU

CHAPTER FIVE — 25
    THE GREAT WEALTH TRANSFER

CHAPTER SIX — 33
    JESUS IS THE LAST MAN STANDING

CHAPTER SEVEN — 38
    BREAKING THE SPIRIT OF DEBT!

CHAPTER EIGHT — 48
    HOW TO LIVE IN THE BLESSING AND ENJOY LIFE

CHAPTER NINE — 55
    HOW GOD TAKES WHAT YOU HAVE AND TURNS IT INTO WHAT YOU NEED

INTRODUCTION

There are many of God's Children who are living far below their potential that is available in Christ Jesus. It reminds me of the story that I read of a young man who came from England to work in the gold fields in California. He struck it rich and found gold.

He bought a first class passage for his father to come over to the United States. Several days into the voyage, the Captain noticed that the man had not come to dine at his table. He sent the purser to see if the old man was alright. Knocking on the cabin door, the purser heard the old man's voice. *"Come in"*. When the purser entered the cabin he saw the old man sitting eating crackers and cheese. *"Sir, the Captain sent me to enquire as to your health?"* The old man declared that he was fine. The purser asked him why he had not joined the Captain for dinner during the last several days. The old man hung his head down and said, *"I cannot afford the meals so that is why I am eating these crackers and cheese."*

The purser took the old man's passage ticket and said, *"Look! The meals are included in your travel and this is a First Class ticket, you are to sit at the Captain's table."* The old man did not know what was available to him. Everything that he needed was in the purchased ticket. He was eating crackers and cheese when he could have had steak and potatoes. He did not have to lack because his son had paid for the best care for his Dad.

Your elder brother Jesus has paid for your care in this life and that which is to come. When you understand what belongs to you as a child of God then you too will sit at the Captain's table with the Lord.

– Ted Shuttlesworth

CHAPTER ONE
GOD WORKS FROM THE INSIDE OUT

Centuries ago, eighteen beans were sealed into a little earthen pot and placed in an Indian burial site in eastern Utah. The beans were discovered by a rancher who turned them over to a horticulturist in Monticello, Utah, to develop. They were planted and those eighteen beans yielded forty pounds of beans, in the fall of 1957.

Three years later, in the summer of 1960, those eighteen beans yielded approximately 80 acres of lush green bushes, growing in rows A HALF MILE LONG! This story illustrates the power of life that is in a seed.

The seed that is not planted is not doing the world any good. The unrealized HARVEST was because of a failure to sow. Jesus said, **"Except a CORN of wheat fall into the ground and die, it abideth ALONE." John 12:24**

The seed has the power of increase in itself.

YOUR next financial harvest is contained in the seed that you sow today!

YOUR harvest is the *spirit of multiplication* released or manifested.

YOUR seed can take you from financial hardship to blessing.

Our financial seeds come from God. Only God can make a seed. Your harvest is a miracle! Although scientists have developed hybrid seeds they have never developed an original seed in their laboratories. The Bible says that,

YOU WILL BE MADE RICH IN EVERY WAY so that you can be generous on every occasion, and through us your generosity will result in thanksgiving to God." 2 Corinthians 9:10-11 NIV

God will always do more for you than you can do for Him. God wants us to have abundance in every area of our lives!

The Great Exchange

"For ye know the grace of our Lord Jesus Christ, that though he was RICH, yet for your sakes he became POOR, that ye through his poverty might be rich." 2 Corinthians 8:9

Jesus was not *"spiritually poor."* The Bible tells us that; **"for God giveth not the Spirit by measure unto HIM." John 3:34** Whereas; you and I only have a measure of faith. **Romans 12:7**

A man who is *"spiritually poor"* could not open the eyes of the blind, make the deaf to hear, and the lame to walk. No, this is not talking about a lack of spiritual power. Jesus was not poor spiritually.

The Apostle Paul shows us that Jesus humbled or emptied Himself of His Divine Riches and took on the form of a servant. **Philippians 2:5-8** It was Jesus that said, **"The foxes have holes, and the birds of the air have nests; but the Son of man hath not where to lay his head." Matthew 8:20**

Jesus had a home in Capernaum. **Matthew 9:7** Yet we know as

He traveled with His disciples that He stayed in the wilderness, by the seashore, and in the mountains. The Son of God had become the Son of man.

This then refers to a Divine Exchange. God's Glory was placed into *"seed-form"* and He identified with you and me that we might have an ABUNDANT LIFE.

The first promise to all mankind was the promise of a seed!

"And I will put enmity between thee and the woman, and between thy seed and HER SEED; it shall bruise thy head, and thou shalt bruise his heel." Genesis 3:15

Jesus was the seed of the woman. Jesus is God's Seed. The foundation of truth about the power of the seed is that God gave HIS ALL! It was His only Son. Now look at all the sons and daughters God has. That one Seed has produced a mighty Harvest of souls!

The Widow and the Rich Men

There is a story in the Bible of a poor widow who gave everything she had to God's Work.

"And Jesus sat over against the treasury, and beheld how the people cast money into the treasury: and many that were RICH CAST in much.

And there came a certain poor widow, and she threw in two mites, which make a farthing.

And he called unto him his disciples, and saith unto them, Verily I say unto you, That this poor widow HATH CAST more in, than all they which have cast into the treasury:

For all they did cast in of their abundance; but she of her want did cast in all that she had, even all her living."

Mark 12:41-44

The rich gave *some* of their wealth. The poor widow gave ALL!

W.E. Vine's Exposition on New Testament Words, defines the word, *"cast"* in reference to the rich in verse 41 and the word *"cast"* in verse 43 where Jesus comments, **"this poor widow hath CAST more in"** differently.

Literally, the translation of verse 41 reads, *"the rich threw"*. The translation of verse 43 where Jesus comments, **"this poor widow hath cast"** is the word *"put"* or *"placed with care."*

The rich threw. The woman put or placed with care her offering.

The Amplified Bible bears out this translation: **"And He called His disciples [to Him] and said to them, Truly and surely I tell you, this widow, [she who is] poverty-stricken has PUT in more than all those contributing to the treasury."**

More can be less. God judges our giving by what is kept! Today's blessing was yesterday's seed! Jesus taught His disciples that what people gave was more important than what they kept. That poor widow was setting herself up to be rich and the rich were setting themselves up to be poor!

"There is that scattereth, and yet increaseth; and there is that withholdeth more than is meet, but it tendeth to poverty.

"The liberal soul shall be made fat; and he that watereth shall be watered also himself." Proverbs 11:24, 25

Years ago, I planted an apple tree next to my driveway. The day I put it in the ground a car hit it. It was still small. My neighbor saw it and said, *"Don't worry the stress on the tree will help to produce more fruit."* This taught me a valuable lesson about God's Creation. Stress brings fruit! Learn how to place the pressure on the seed and take the pressure off of yourself.

That tree has borne fruit every year since then. Hundreds of apples fill the limbs of that tree every fall. I remind myself that every apple is filled with seeds and each seed has a tree in it! God shows us through nature that He is a God of Great Abundance and that He blesses the seed.

The miracle that you need is in your seed!

CHAPTER TWO
GOD'S KEY TO MULTIPLYING MONEY

"While the earth remaineth, SEEDTIME AND HARVEST, and cold and heat, and summer and winter, and day and night shall not cease." Genesis 8:22

It takes faith to give to God! Our giving is an act of our love for God and our trust in His Promises of provision for our lives. *Our financial success is determined by our understanding of giving!*

There was an old minister that I used to go and hear preach. I loved the wisdom and faith that flowed out of his spirit. It was very refreshing to me. He said that after having been in the ministry for over 50 years, that he had concluded that more people failed when it came to faith for finances than anything else.

He was amazed at how people wanted the Lord to bless them financially but they had not sown any seed. I determined in my heart that I would always teach on the law of sowing and reaping at least one night in the meetings that I held. People need help financially and the Word of God holds their answer!

Obeying God with your giving is the KEY to prosperity. If you want God to give to you, *you've got to do something first!* Jesus taught that we must give to receive.

"GIVE, and it shall be given unto you; good measure, pressed down, and shaken together, and running over, shall men give into your bosom. For with the same measure that ye mete withal it shall be measured to you again." Luke 6:38

The devil does not want you to give anything to God. He knows God will give back to you in a *greater measure* than what you gave.

You and I are people of faith. We are in this world but we are not of this world. We are like Abraham, **"For he looked for a city which hath foundations, whose builder and maker is God. Hebrews 11:10**

There are two economic systems.
There is the world's economy and God's economy.

The world's economy is based on fear and greed.
God's financial system is based on faith and abundance.

The world's economy goes up and down.
God's economy is based on increase.

We Prosper by Sowing and Reaping

YOUR *next financial harvest is determined in the seed YOU sow today!*

Only what you give can God multiply back to you again. The Lord wants you to receive a bountiful blessing. He wants you to reap a great harvest in your life. Faithfulness brings God's financial blessings into your life. Keep sowing because you will see a harvest from your seed.

"**And let us not be weary in well doing: for IN DUE SEASON WE SHALL REAP, if we faint not."** Galatians 6:9

The Bible refers to our money as *"seed."*

"But this I say, He which soweth sparingly shall reap also sparingly; and he which soweth bountifully shall reap also bountifully.

Every man according as he purposeth in his heart, SO LET HIM GIVE; not grudgingly, or of necessity: for God loveth A CHEERFUL GIVER. 2 Corinthians 9:6-7

Now he that ministereth SEED to the sower both minister bread for your food, and multiply YOUR SEED SOWN, and increase the fruits of your righteousness;" 2 Corinthians 9:10

The apostle Paul taught that our money is the seed we sow. It can be sown **"sparingly"** or it can be sown **"bountifully."**

God Has Promised to do Three Things When We Give to Him

First, He has promised to give us more seed to sow. When someone tells me that they have nothing to give then I know that they are not a giver. He gives **"SEED to the SOWER."**

When I was eighteen I left home and went away to Bible school. My father told me to *"Trust God!"* He wanted me to learn how to believe God for money. The day came when I needed to do laundry. I had no money. It was time to *trust God!*

I decided that I would get up early the next day and go to the prayer room and ask the Lord to give me some money. I wrote down my giving Scriptures on index cards. When 6:00 A.M. came, I headed across to the prayer room in the Temple.

I was all set to pray when the Lord spoke to me. *"You can have the five dollars, go ahead and go now."* He did not even let me read

Him those Scriptures. I got up and went outside to go over to the dining hall for breakfast when a young woman stopped me.

"Who's the best car washer on campus? I need my car washed for the wedding on Saturday." I told her I would wash her car. She then reached in her purse and pulled out five dollars! She told me that she wanted to pay me now so that I would not forget to do it. God bless Lorna. She's in Heaven now.

I stood there with the five dollars in my hand. If I had waited and prayed all my Scriptures I would have missed the blessing. Then the Lord spoke to my spirit again. He said, *"Fifty cents of that is Mine."* I promised Him that I would put my tithe (the tenth) in on Sunday. Just as clear these words came up in my spirit, *"You wanted your money today. I want my money today!"*

I went across the street to a donut shop to break the $5 but they said I had to buy donuts or coffee. Then I went from there across the street to a little store and bought some soap powder and razor blades.

I ran back to the Temple auditorium. They had a golden bowl that was left on the communion table for tithes. I walked down to put those two quarters in. When I looked in, there was other money there. I dropped them in and turned to go up the aisle of the church when I heard the words that changed my life forever.

"If you give me the rest of your money you will never lack for anything the rest of your life."

I can still feel the anointing on those words. So I turned back and put that dollar in the golden bowl. Remember, I was only eighteen at the time and from that day to this I have never lacked for anything in my life. Bless His Name Forever!

God gave me seed to sow! He wants to give you seed to sow

as well. Then He says that He will bless our **"seed sown."** *The multiplying power is on the seed that we give and not that which we keep.*

Finally, He declares that He will cause **"increase"** to come to us. However, we determined the size of what we reap by the amount we sow. We choose to sow **"sparingly"** or **"bountifully."**

My seed sown guarantees me that I have a future. When you cooperate with the *law of sowing and reaping* then you get into God's Cycle of Blessing. It will work for the rest of your life if you will work it.

The Lord knows what amount of money you will need in the future. When you give what the Lord shows you then it will be multiplied. That is why it is important to obey God in our giving because it will affect our destiny.

CHAPTER THREE
SEND NOW PROSPERITY!

How would you like to have a bank account that never goes empty? What if you could write a check for whatever you wanted and still have more than enough left over? A recent report that I read stated that, *"Many people are only one paycheck from bankruptcy."*

I immediately wondered, *"How many of them are God's Children?"*

There is a way out of financial trouble. There is a road to blessing. Perhaps you are tired of financial pressure or worry about how you are going to pay your bills. Your prayers for help seemingly go unanswered.

"Save now, I beseech thee, O LORD: O LORD, I beseech thee, SEND NOW PROSPERITY." Psalm 118:25

This was the prayer of King David as he prepared to take the throne of Israel. When David asked God to send him prosperity he had nothing in the natural. Yet, before King David died he gave one of the largest offerings to build God a house that is ever recorded in Scripture. No one has ever given this large of an offering even until this day.

David started with nothing but a handful of men **"that was** in DISTRESS, and every one that was in DEBT, and every one that was DISCONTENTED, gathered themselves unto him; and he became a captain over them: and there were with him about four hundred men." 1 Samuel 22:2

God Wants To Be Your Partner

Here is an inspiring *"rags to riches"* story. David was surrounded by a lot of broke folks. **Psalm 118** tells the story of how David found out that God wanted to be his Partner! When he was surrounded by all the Philistine nations *[All nations compassed me about]* and they were trying to prevent him from establishing himself in the kingdom. *[The Lord taketh my part with them that help me]* He was delivered by God's power and used to bring back the glory of God to Israel.

God did send David prosperity! The largest offering ever given to God was from King David. The equivalent of what he gave in today's money would be over ONE BILLION DOLLARS! *(Read this story in 1 Chronicles 29: 1-17)*

Yet, God had so prospered David that he still had great wealth left over at his death. **"And he died in a good old age, full of days, RICHES, and honour: and Solomon his son reigned in his stead." 1 Chronicles 29:28**

YOU need to speak these powerful words over your life.

LORD, SEND ME PROSPERITY NOW!

Faith works in the NOW! The writer of Hebrews records, **"NOW faith is." Hebrews 11:1** You need help now. The bills are due now. You need your financial breakthrough now.

Unlock the Power of THE BLESSING

The first thing you must do is ASK the Lord to send you prosperity now!

Why would God help us financially? What is there in the Word that shows us that He will bring wealth and blessing into our lives? The answer to this question is very important. YOU determine whether you live in plenty and abundance, not God! Jesus taught that you must ask if you want to receive!

"And I say unto you, Ask, and it shall be given you; seek, and ye shall find; knock, and it shall be opened unto you.

For every one that asketh receiveth; and he that seeketh findeth; and to him that knocketh it shall be opened."
Luke 11:9-10

Secondly, you must GIVE offerings to God's Work to have financial increase.

"Honour the LORD with thy substance, and with the firstfruits of all thine increase:

So shall thy barns be filled with plenty, and thy presses shall burst out with new wine." Proverbs 3:9-10

Your substance is your possessions. Everything that you have belongs to God. All that He requires is your first fruits. What you have now is a result of what you gave in the past.

God wants us to live in obedience to His Word. The scripture declares, **"If ye be willing and obedient, ye shall eat the good of the land:" Isaiah 1:19** How many times have we missed God's best for our lives because we were not willing and obedient?

4 Bible Reasons Why God Wants You Wealthy

Perhaps you may be wondering why God wants you to be wealthy and have this prosperity? Maybe you are thinking, *"I just want to pay my bills and have a little extra."* What does the Bible say about why God wants us to enjoy great wealth and prosperity?

1. God wants you to be wealthy to provide for your family.

"But if any provide not for his own, and specially for those of his own house, he hath denied the faith, and is worse than an infidel."

1 Timothy 5:8

2. God wants you to be wealthy to help the poor and needy.

"He that hath pity upon the poor lendeth unto the LORD; and that which he hath given will he pay him again." **Proverbs 19:17**

3. God wants you to be wealthy for His pleasure.

"Let them shout for joy, and be glad, that favour my righteous cause: yea, let them say continually, Let the LORD be magnified, which hath pleasure in the prosperity of his servant." **Psalm 35:27**

4. God wants you to be wealthy so that His perfect will may be done in your life.

"Beloved, I wish above all things that thou mayest prosper and be in health, even as thy soul prospereth." **3 John 2**

The Lord is well pleased when His Children do well. It is His desire that we prosper in every area of our life. We are blessed to bless others, our families, and those who truly need help. Get ready for the Lord to use you mightily in these last days!

We must renew our minds to the Bible fact that wealth is a direct result of our understanding of God's Purpose and His Plan to show forth His Power to every generation. It is THE BLESSING that contains all that we will ever need.

When you purpose in your heart that you will not lack but you will have God's Best, then you will see a supernatural turn around in your finances. What a joy it is to serve the Lord! The knowledge of Him brings a release of wisdom in our daily lives.

"Happy is the man that findeth wisdom, and the man that getteth understanding.

For the merchandise of it is better than the merchandise of silver, and the gain thereof than fine gold.

She is more precious than rubies: and all the things thou canst desire are not to be compared unto her.

Length of days is in her right hand; and in her left hand RICHES AND HONOUR." Proverbs 3:13-16

CHAPTER FOUR
THE BLESSING IS ALREADY IN YOU

GOD wants you to remember that HE bought your last meal. GOD has instructed me to remind you that HE purchased your clothes. It is God who will help you pay your bills and GOD who wants to bless you with a home. GOD said you would never lack even for a loaf of bread. (**Deuteronomy 8:6-14**)

There is one anointing that GOD gives that many ministers are embarrassed to teach about! It is the anointing that GOD gives to get wealth. That anointing is the ability, the capacity, the force, and the power of God to make something work.

"But thou shalt remember the LORD thy God: for it is he that giveth thee POWER TO GET WEALTH, that he may establish his covenant which he sware unto thy fathers, as it is this day." Deuteronomy 8:18

God has an anointing that will bring wealth to you. There is an anointing to get wealth and there are six words that tell us why God gives us this ability:

"THAT HE MAY ESTABLISH HIS COVENANT"

There is a Divine Purpose in prosperity. It is that we remember to use our monies to help establish God's Covenant on the earth. *We are blessed to be a blessing.* That is the covenant in its simplest form. My money is to help bring souls to Christ.

How the Lord Taught Me the Value of Money

"WHICH IS GREATER, SOULS OR MONEY?" One morning, in my room, the Lord spoke these words to me very clearly.

I said, "Lord, souls are more important."

Then after some time, I heard these words again, "WHICH IS GREATER, SOULS OR MONEY?" To be honest with you I felt a little hurt by this. Did the Lord think that I was mercenary?

I had shut myself up in this closet to pray and fast for a greater working of miracles in my life and ministry. We had seen many deaf healed in the meetings. However, there were not many blind healed. I could only think of two people that had been healed of blindness. I was praying for miracles.

What was this all about? What was the Lord saying to me? Then, I heard it for the third time. "WHICH IS GREATER, SOULS OR MONEY?" I said, "Lord souls are more important than money!"

The next words changed my thinking forever. "IF YOU DO NOT HAVE FAITH FOR THE LESSER WHICH IS MONEY THAN HOW CAN YOU HAVE FAITH FOR THE GREATER WHICH ARE THE SOULS?"

I knew then that I must develop my faith for money if I wanted to reach many souls. There is an anointing that God gives that produces wealth. This wealth has purpose and is targeted specifically to bring this Divine Plan into full manifestation in your life.

There are three reasons why this power is available to you as a child of God, today! God does not change! *We are the seed of*

Abraham and heirs to this promise. The Covenant of God is forever.

God spoke to the prophet Malachi:

"FOR I AM THE LORD, I CHANGE NOT" Malachi 3:6

If God said in **Deuteronomy 8:18** that He gave us power to get wealth, over three thousand years ago, and since He cannot change, then HE MUST STILL GIVE THAT SAME POWER TODAY!

God promised Abraham and all the fathers of the covenant certain blessings. What Abraham received in promise and what Moses and the children of Israel were reminded of by covenant is still true today. GOD CANNOT CHANGE!

Our Inheritance

The Apostle Paul taught that the child of God's inheritance was a part of the promise given to Abraham in covenant.

"Know ye therefore that they which are of faith, the same are the children of Abraham. Galatians 3:7

"That the blessing of Abraham might come on the Gentiles through Jesus Christ; that we might receive the promise of the Spirit through faith." Galatians 3:14

"And if ye be Christ's, then are ye Abraham's seed, and heirs according to the promise." Galatians 3:29

Well, I am not ashamed to say that I am Christ's. Plainly, the New Testament teaches that Christians are the "CHILDREN OF ABRAHAM" and we are the "HEIRS" of God's Covenant in **Deuteronomy 8:18!**

Jesus admonished us of the direct link between His return

and the establishing of the kingdom through the preaching of the gospel in every nation.

"And this gospel of the kingdom shall be preached in all the world for a witness unto all nations; and then shall the end come." Matthew 24:14

GOD GIVES WEALTH AND THE POWER TO GET IT SO THAT THE GOSPEL MIGHT BE PREACHED IN ALL THE NATIONS OF THE WORLD!

God wants to accomplish this more than you or I do. Did you ever stop to think what it costs, each day, all over the world, to get the Gospel out? Well, the Lord knows how much that bill is. GOD knows and because He is the GOD who supplies every need He releases the finances necessary to get the job done. However, there is the human element that is involved.

What if God releases the wealth but His children hold on to it because they have forgotten to remember that it is God Who gives power to get wealth? Then the Gospel is hindered due to lack of finances. *Remember, we are blessed to be a blessing!*

If you seek first God's kingdom then the power to get wealth will be used properly. Then the Lord will add to us other things that we need. **"But seek ye first the kingdom of God, and his righteousness; and all these things shall be added unto you." Matthew 6:33**

The Apostle Paul had this revelation that Jesus has already blessed us and given us an inheritance. You are already living in THE BLESSING. The knowledge of what Jesus has already accomplished gives us faith to be blessed.

"Blessed be the God and Father of our Lord Jesus Christ, who HATH BLESSED US with all spiritual blessings in heavenly

places in Christ:" Ephesians 1:3

"In whom also we HAVE OBTAINED AN INHERITANCE."
Ephesians 1:11

"And HATH put all things under His feet, and gave Him to be the head over all things TO THE CHURCH,

Which is his body, the fulness of him that filleth all in all."
Ephesians 1:22, 23

I call this the *"past tense"* of the Gospel. Jesus has already provided everything that we will ever need in this life through His triumphant victory over the *"god of this world."*

We are not going to get an inheritance. We already have obtained an inheritance through Jesus Christ. He is the Head over all things and that includes our finances.

That abundant life is now given to us and it is up to us to enforce that victory that Jesus gave us when He destroyed the devil's power through His death, resurrection, and ascension. Praise God!

CHAPTER FIVE
THE GREAT WEALTH TRANSFER

"Believe in the Lord your God, so shall ye be established; BELIEVE HIS PROPHETS, so shall ye PROSPER." 2 Chronicles 20:20

There is a connection between the anointed prophetic word and prosperity in the Bible. Do we live by the prophetic word? If you consider the Word of God to be a revelation, then the answer is *YES!*

God's Word should govern our lives. The whole Word of God is a prophetic panorama of God's dealing with man.

The Gift of Prophecy in operation is a *supernatural utterance*. It can be spoken over the life of an individual and can be a key that God gives us to live a victorious Christian life.

How God Multiplied My Money

The Tyendinaga Reserve is located in Deseronto, Ontario. It was a hot night in August and I was sitting under a canvas tent with hundreds of people. The evangelist was receiving an offering for the Native Bible College. He began to prophesy. *"If you will give God the biggest thing you have on you tonight He will bless you back at least ten-fold."*

I knew that I only had enough money to get back to my friends in Toronto. There was $22 in my pocket, two one-dollar bills and a twenty-dollar bill. My first thought was, *"That's the devil trying to trick me out of my twenty dollars!"*

So I went up and put the two one-dollar bills in. Then I went back and sat down. I felt miserable. I kept hearing this voice, *"Give the twenty."* I began to rebuke the devil. Then it dawned on me, the devil did not want me to give to help spread the Gospel. I knew I did not want to give it. That only left the Lord's Voice.

I went back up to give the twenty. The evangelist saw me coming and said, *"God gotcha didn't He!"* I felt like reaching in and taking the twenty back but I knew the Bible says, **"God loves a cheerful giver."** 2 Corinthians 9:7 So I smiled and went back to my seat. That was all the money I had.

The service was over and they were turning the lights out. I was headed to my car when an older man came up to me. *"Here son, God told me to bless you!"* He tucked something in my suit pocket. I knew the sound of paper money. I looked for a light to see what he had given me. There was a street light on across the field and I took off running.

When I got under the light I pulled two brand-new one hundred dollar bills out of my pocket! It was exactly ten times the twenty dollars that I had put in the offering. Then I knew God really does speak through men of God. I got a little upset. If I had obeyed the Lord I would have had $202 dollars! The Word of God works!

That's why Paul encouraged Timothy to take advantage of the prophetic words in his life and to use them as weapons in spiritual warfare.

"This charge I commit unto thee, son Timothy, according to the PROPHECIES which went before on thee, that thou BY

THEM mightest war a good warfare;" 1 Timothy 1:18

Wealth Transfer Prophesied

God always gave a prophetic word before He transferred wealth into the hands of His children. He prophesied blessing to Abram.

"And I will make of thee a great nation, and I WILL BLESS THEE, and make thy name great; and thou shalt be a blessing: Genesis 12:2

God leads His people to wealth! Abram obeyed and went out from the Ur of the Chaldees. God took him to a place that He gave him as an inheritance. "**And Abram was very RICH in cattle, in silver, and in gold.**" Genesis 13:2

Abram's *"wealthy place"* was contained in the prophetic words that God spoke to him. "**But thou broughtest us out into a WEALTHY PLACE.**" Psalm 66:12

The key to Abram's prosperity, who later was called Abraham, was his obedience to the prophetic word of God in his life. "**By faith Abraham, when he was called to go out into a place which he should after receive for an inheritance, OBEYED; and he went out, not knowing whither he went.**" Hebrews 11:8

We can expect to receive the riches that God has for us when we are obedient to His Word. "**So then they which be of FAITH are BLESSED with faithful Abraham.**" Galatians 3:9

God Prophesied Deliverance with Wealth to Israel

The Lord prophesied to Moses concerning the future of the

people of Israel. He instructed Moses that He was going to cause Pharaoh to let them go. The Lord commanded Moses, as the leader, to speak to the people about taking the Egyptians' wealth with them.

"And I will give this people FAVOUR in the sight of the Egyptians: and it shall come to pass, that, when ye go, ye shall not go EMPTY." Exodus 3:21

God's Favor guaranteed a full supply! He was not going to let His people go out **"empty."** They had endured slavery for hundreds of years. The Bible says that they had built the **"treasure cities"** for the Pharaohs. **Exodus 1:11** Yet, they did not share the treasure! This is how the devil would like to operate in your life and in this Nation. He would like to get you to work like a slave and then steal your blessing.

Favor is a gift of God! God told Moses that, **"I will give this people favor."**

How did God give His people **"favor"**? He gave them the wealth of the nation! He transferred the riches of Egypt from the hands of Pharaoh's crowd and gave it to His children. This is the first Bible record of a *"wealth transfer."* God did it!

This word came to pass and its' fulfillment is found in **Psalm 105:37**:

"He brought them forth also with SILVER AND GOLD: and there was not one feeble person among their tribes."

God's Word Prophesies Wealth Coming Into Your Hands

I believe in the end-times, which the Bible seems to indicate as a time of economic uncertainty, that God is getting ready to transfer great amounts of money to His children that will use it to help spread the Gospel of Jesus Christ!

"This is the portion of a wicked man with God, and the heritage of oppressors, which they shall receive of the Almighty.

Though he heap up silver as the dust, and prepare raiment as the clay;

He may prepare it, BUT THE JUST SHALL PUT IT ON, AND THE INNOCENT SHALL DIVIDE THE SILVER." Job 27:13, 16,17

"For God giveth to a man that is good in his sight wisdom, and knowledge, and joy: but to the SINNER he giveth travail, to gather and to heap up, THAT HE MAY GIVE TO HIM THAT IS GOOD BEFORE GOD. This also is vanity and vexation of spirit." Ecclesiastes 2:26

"A good man leaveth an inheritance to his children's children: and THE WEALTH OF THE SINNER IS LAID UP FOR THE JUST." Proverbs 13:22

The Amplified Bible translates this verse as, "**The wealth of the heathen will EVENTUALLY find its way into the hands of the righteous.**"

The children of God are going to eventually find great wealth coming into their hands. We have a covenant agreement through Jesus Christ for the promised blessing. **"And if ye be Christ's, then are ye Abraham's seed, and HEIRS according to the promise."** Galatians 3:29

The wealth of the wicked belongs to the child of God. There is a difference between covenant and covetousness! When you understand your covenant rights through Jesus Christ, then and only then, can you properly understand the role that money plays in your life.

Blessing or Curse?

Poverty, is it a blessing or is it a curse? There are some who teach that the Bible says you may take a *vow of poverty* as a spiritual expression of your faith and obedience to God. This is of course is not scriptural and has no Biblical basis.

No, poverty is a curse. The *spirit of poverty* affects the condition of the mind. It then manifests in the lives of people as lack. God first dealt with this issue in **Deuteronomy 28:15-17:**

"But it shall come to pass, if thou wilt not hearken unto the voice of the LORD thy God, to observe to do all his commandments and his statutes which I command thee this day; that all these curses shall come upon thee, and overtake thee:

Cursed shalt thou be in the city, and cursed shalt thou be in the field.

Cursed shall be thy basket and thy store." [This could be your checkbook and savings account.]

We understand then that poverty is a part of the Curse of the Law.

I am convinced that many in the Body of Christ have grown indifferent concerning the Law of Sowing and Reaping and the advancement of the work of God. There are those who think that it is not spiritual to focus our attention on money or giving to the work of God.

There are some people who believe that money is evil. Money is not evil, but rather, the love of money. **"For THE LOVE OF MONEY is the root of all evil: which while some coveted after, they have erred from the faith,** *and* **pierced themselves through with many sorrows."** 1 Timothy 6:10

There is a money revival! While in prayer, this understanding came to my spirit. The Lord is releasing the money to get the Gospel out for the end-time harvest of souls. We need to learn how to move into this area of Divine Blessing.

"Praise ye the LORD. Blessed is the man that feareth the LORD that delighteth greatly in his commandments.

His seed shall be mighty upon earth: the generation of the upright shall be blessed.

WEALTH AND RICHES SHALL BE IN HIS HOUSE: and his righteousness endureth for ever." Psalm 112:1-3

A Homeless Woman Receives A House In Florida

R.W. Schambach had his tent up in the Bronx. We were holding two services a day. It was in one of the day services that a homeless woman came under the tent and heard the Gospel for the first time.

She answered the altar call and I ministered to her. She said to me that she was Jewish and that she did not know that if you became a Christian that God would give you a house!

I didn't know that either. The message that day was about how God would take care of you if you would trust Him. Some how in her mind that translated into the thought that Jesus would give her a house. I didn't want to discourage her so I told her I would believe that God would give her a home.

The next night, she came under the tent happy and waving a yellow manila envelope. *"I got the house!"* She explained to me how that when her mother died her sister got all of the money and house. It left her homeless. She had been living in a homeless shelter and sleeping under the bridge.

Apparently, her sister became convicted and hired a detective to track down her sister. As the Lord would have it, he found her the day after she came to the altar. She told my wife and I that she could not stay for the meeting because her sister had bought her a plane ticket to Fort Lauderdale and she was leaving that night. The ticket and the keys to her new house were in the envelope!

I learned a very powerful lesson in God's Strategy of bringing THE BLESSING into the lives of everyday people. She had told us that if the Lord would give her a house that she would become a Christian. What is a house compared to a soul? Nothing! The greater lesson was that God will do whatever it takes for lost souls to be saved.

The Lord loves you as well, my friend. You are His Child and He cares for you greatly. Do not allow the devil to lie to you. It is God Who blesses His Children. The Lord has a blessing for you today.

CHAPTER SIX
JESUS IS THE LAST MAN STANDING

The last song ended and now there were 50 pair of eyes watching me. The youth pastor looked at me and nodded. I had been praying that the Lord would somehow move supernaturally on everyone so that I did not have to go forward to the platform.

My legs felt shaky and my mouth was dry. I climbed those stairs as slowly as possible. I had prayed and studied. Now it was time for me to preach my first sermon. That night, in Kenosha, Wisconsin, the Lord started me in the ministry. I was 14 years old.

Forty years later, the Pennsylvania countryside was rolling by the windows of my car. It was a sunny day in May. I was enjoying the view from the passenger's seat. I had received a call earlier that week from California from Oral Robert's secretary. I called her back from the car that day. We began to talk about a few matters and then I asked her how Dr. Roberts was doing. She said, *"He is here! Would you like to talk to him?"* The next thing that I knew Oral Roberts was talking with me on the cell phone.

"My Brother, I love you!" These were his first words. Then for the next half-hour he exhorted me, prophesied to me and then prayed for me. I listened and wrote down what he said as fast as I could write. It was these words that exploded in my spirit.

"Ted, I pray Luke 10:2 over you. Jesus is the Lord of the Harvest! He is the Lord of YOUR harvest. May He bless you spiritually, physically, and financially. From this day forward I command my blessing to come on you!" When he said that, the Presence of the Lord filled that car! It was real!

I thought back to that night that I first preached. The title of my message was, *"The Lord of the Harvest"* and my text was from **Luke 10:2**

"Therefore said he unto them, The harvest truly is great, but the labourers are few: pray ye therefore the LORD OF THE HARVEST, that he would send forth labourers into his harvest."

What a wonderful Jesus! I had been battling thoughts of failure and frustration. Wondering if the Lord would use me in this end-time harvest for souls. My faith seemed weak and a tiredness of soul that only warriors who have stood on the front lines understand suddenly evaporated and the power of Heaven filled my heart.

Jesus let me know, through that precious man of God, that He was there when I was a boy and He is still with me as a man. Jesus is the Lord of the Harvest!

The Great End-Time Harvest

Jesus gave this wonderful promise and challenge to seventy of His disciples just before He sent them into the towns and cities where He would come. Clearly, the *harvest* of **Luke 10:2** is SOULS.

Jesus told them to go into the houses of the people and to heal their sick. Their message was a simple one. **"The kingdom of God is come nigh unto you." Luke 10:9** Those men went and began to labor in the harvest of souls. When they returned back to Jesus they were filled with joy. **"Lord, even the devils are subject unto us through thy name." Luke 10:17**

The end-time harvest is the souls of men and women who are bound by the devil. They are sin-sick and physically sick. Jesus promised to send anointed laborers into what He said was *His harvest*.

I am reminded of the words of Isaiah's vision, **"Also I heard the voice of the Lord, saying, Whom shall I send, and who will go for us? Then said I, Here am I; send me." Isaiah 6:8**

The greatest debt that we have is that of the Gospel. We owe the world the story of Jesus. Recently, I heard an older minister prophesy and speak of a vision that the Lord gave Him. There were two things he mentioned.

First, that we need to get ready for the second coming of Jesus Christ. Secondly, we need to increase our understanding of sowing and reaping financially. He made this statement, *"It's time to sow to God toward the Second Coming of Christ"*.

I immediately thought of **James 5**. This is the chapter that deals with the world's financial system in light of the last days and the coming of the Lord.

"Your gold and silver is cankered; and the rust of them shall be a witness against you, and shall eat your flesh as it were fire. Ye have heaped TREASURE TOGETHER FOR THE LAST DAYS." James 5:3

"Be patient therefore, brethren, unto THE COMING OF THE LORD. Behold, the husbandman waiteth for the precious fruit of the earth, and hath long patience for it, until he receive the early and latter rain.

Be ye also patient; stablish your hearts: for THE COMING OF THE LORD draweth nigh." James 5:7-8

James the pastor of the church in Jerusalem prophesied that something would happen to the gold and silver in the end-time financial system. *Whatever shaking out that is coming will take place in the last days and before the coming of Jesus Christ!*

It was Jesus who taught us that, **"Ye cannot serve God and mammon." Matthew 6:24**

Mammon, in the Bible speaks of the world's system of finance. It is the world's wealth and riches. However, He said we could use them for good. **"If therefore ye have not been faithful in the unrighteous mammon, who will commit to your trust the true riches?" Luke 16:11** God has a financial system as well for His children.

The world's system runs by fear and greed. God's system functions through giving and receiving.

The true riches are the souls the **"precious fruit of the earth"**. Jesus is seen as the husbandman, the great Lord of the Harvest watching over the **"precious fruit"** which are the souls of the end-time harvest.

A harvest requires a seed be planted. If there is no seed then there can be no harvest!

The Scripture reminds us that there is **"a time to plant, and a time to pluck up that which is planted;" Ecclesiastes 3:2**

There are then two harvests that Jesus the Lord of the Harvest is watching over; the harvest of lost souls that have received the seed of the Word of God and your financial harvest that was planted in the good ground of soul winning.

End-time wealth for the end-time harvest of SOULS!

Jesus will be standing while the nations of the world are falling. He stands over the harvest for lost souls and He stands over your financial harvest as well. He will not be moved and He will not allow you to lack if you will trust in Him. You should keep sowing no matter how things look.

"If the clouds be full of rain, they empty themselves upon the earth: and if the tree fall toward the south, or toward the north, in the place where the tree falleth, there it shall be.

He that observeth the wind shall not sow; and he that regardeth the clouds shall not reap.

As thou knowest not what is the way of the spirit, nor how the bones do grow in the womb of her that is with child; even so thou knowest not the works of God who maketh all.

In the morning sow thy seed, and in the evening withold not thy hand: for thou knowest not whether shall prosper, either this or that, or whether they both shall be alike good." Ecclesiastes 11:3-6

The devil will try to get you to operate through your natural senses. If you look at what is going on in the natural you will become discouraged and fearful. However, if you keep your eyes on the Lord you will always succeed in everything you do. THE BLESSING works all the time, every time, and in every age. God's Economic Principles cannot be affected by the world's economic ups and downs!

CHAPTER SEVEN
BREAKING THE SPIRIT OF DEBT!

God wants you out of debt! The Apostle Paul reminds us that we are to; **"Owe no man any thing," Romans 13:8** There is a desire in my heart to help God's people understand the need for financial freedom. When you consider that a person's debt enslaves them **"the borrower is SERVANT to the LENDER." Proverbs 22:7** and brings ultimate destruction to them **"the DESTRUCTION of the POOR is their POVERTY." Proverbs 10:15** then it is vital that we be free from the spirit of debt.

Jesus taught us that it is Satan that is behind the power of destruction. **"The thief cometh not, but for to steal, and to kill, and to DESTROY" John 10:10** I believe that when you are in debt you are not just dealing with the money that you owe; but *a demonic power designed to enslave you and destroy you with debt could be at work!*

I am convinced that it takes a supernatural anointing and a proper understanding of the Word of God to enjoy financial blessing. The first anointing Jesus claimed to have was **"to preach the gospel to the POOR". Luke 4:18**

Jesus said that before He brought healing to the broken-hearted, and before He brought deliverance to the captive, and even before He brought sight to the blind, that HE FIRST WAS ANOINTED

TO PREACH TO THE POOR!

Smith Wigglesworth's Testimony

Smith Wigglesworth was a mighty evangelist from England. He began as a plumber and finished as a worldwide minister of the Gospel. Where you are now is not where you will finish. The Lord taught Wigglesworth the importance of living in THE BLESSING. Smith Wigglesworth used his finances to help feed the poor so that he could preach about Jesus Christ's Healing Power.

"But when thou makest a feast, call the poor, the maimed, the lame, the blind:

And thou shalt be blessed; for they cannot recompense thee: for thou shalt be recompensed at the resurrection of the just." Luke 14:13-14

Smith Wigglesworth tells the story of how this scripture launched him in the healing ministry.

"I engaged two people to go out and find all the needy, the sick, and the afflicted and I gave them tickets inviting them to a banquet and entertainment at the Bowland Street Mission. That sight was beyond all description. All around the mission there were wheelchairs and people on crutches and the blind were being led. This was the best day in my life up to that point. I wept and wept and wept...because of the great need and for joy at the opportunity."

Wigglesworth tells that after feeding them a first class meal, he gave them entertainment. It was the testimonies of those that had been healed in the mission. Then he shouted, *"Who wants to be healed?"* "My friend, they came out of wheelchairs, the power of God shook the place. One young man encased in an iron suit was anointed with oil. He cried out, *"Papa, Papa, it's going all over me! It's going all over me!"* Wigglesworth testified, *"He was loosened that day and made absolutely free!"*

God's Financial Systems That Break the Spirit of Debt

When GOD promised to give us power to get wealth HE also gave us three different financial systems that would provide the means whereby HE might bless us with that wealth. *(Full supply)* Do you know what they are?

1. The Atonement Offering

God spoke to Moses concerning the salvation of the souls of the people. He instructed him that once a year there would be a *Day of Atonement.* The blood of the sacrifice of bulls and heifers and goats would be offered up. That blood that was shed would cover the sins of the people of Israel for one whole year. That day was called *The Day of Atonement.*

God declared, *"It's going to cost my people money to pay for the sacrifices."* He even told them how much to give to buy the sacrifice.

"The rich shall not give more, and the poor shall not give less than half a shekel, when they give an offering unto the LORD, to make an atonement for your souls." Exodus 30:15

So the Atonement Offering was given once a year to provide a covering for the sin of the people. It cost a *half a shekel.* The day came when the *Atonement offering* was not enough! Isaiah prophesied that that day would come,

"Ho, every one that thirsteth, come ye to the waters, and HE THAT HATH NO MONEY; come ye, buy, and eat; yea, come, buy wine and milk without money and without price.

Incline your ear, and come unto me: hear, and your soul shall live; and I WILL MAKE AN EVERLASTING COVENANT WITH YOU, even the sure mercies of David." Isaiah 55:1,3

God did not do away with the *Atonement offering* but He fulfilled by what Jesus did on the Cross! The apostle Peter looking back at that wonderful day taught us;

"Forasmuch as ye know that ye were not redeemed with corruptible things, as SILVER AND GOLD, from your vain conversation received by tradition from your fathers; but with THE PRECIOUS BLOOD OF CHRIST, as of a lamb without blemish and without spot: 1 Peter 1:18-19

I Received a Miracle at the McDonalds in Maine

I was preaching in Northern Maine and New Brunswick in the winter of 1977. The Lord greatly used David and Mary MacIntyre to help me get started in the ministry. I drove from my parents' home in Virginia to northern Maine in February.

The cold blue winter sky held the promise of my future. I was happy and had just enough money to get to these meetings. Brother Mac, as we affectionately call him, believed in me and scheduled me to preach in his church in Hartland, New Brunswick.

That meeting went for four weeks and many were saved and blessed. Then he scheduled me to preach in some youth rallies in Aroostook County, Maine and one in Woodstock, New Brunswick.

I drove back and forth across the border to the meetings in Woodstock. My grandmother lived in Houlton, Maine, so I stayed with her for a few days. It was about a 25-minute drive each night.

Houlton is the last exit on Interstate 95 before you cross over into Canada. There is a McDonalds at that exit. I did not have any extra money to stop after services but I sure could smell those hamburgers and fries as I drove back to my grandmother's house each night.

One night, I decided to stop even though I had no money. I went up to the counter and asked the girl for a cup of water. That was still free in those days. There is a nice fireplace in that McDonalds so I thought I would sit there and enjoy the warmth of it.

When the girl came back she slid a tray across the counter. It had a Big Mac, large fries, and Coke on it. I quickly told her, *"I did not order this."* Secretly, I was ready to take it and run. *"This is not mine."* I said.

Then the manager came over. *"Hello, Brother Shuttlesworth!"* I smelled a blessing coming my way. He said, *"You, don't remember me?"* I did not but I sure wanted to. *"I was in your service last night and came to the altar."*

Then he reached in his shirt pocket and pulled out a red pen and wrote PAID. I said to him, *"Bob, I am going to preach this everywhere I go."* When we could not pay for our sins Jesus paid for it with His Red Blood on the Cross! Praise God!

2. The Offering of the Tithe

"And all the TITHE of the land, whether of the seed of the land, or of the fruit of the tree, is the LORD'S: it is HOLY unto the LORD."

Leviticus 27:30

The tithe is ten per cent of all the money you make.

That means that it belongs to Him. My father and mother taught me as a little boy that ten cents out of every dollar belonged to GOD. The money that I gave in addition to that was my offering. I paid tithes (tenth) and gave my offerings.

Jesus taught that men should *tithe.*

"Woe unto you, scribes and Pharisees, hypocrites! for ye pay TITHE of mint and anise and cummin, and have omitted the weightier matters of the law, judgment, mercy, and faith: THESE OUGHT YE TO HAVE DONE, and not to leave the other undone." Matthew 23:23

TO THE DEGREE THAT YOU HONOR GOD WILL BE TO THE DEGREE THAT GOD WILL HONOR YOU!

Some of our friends who do not believe that *tithing* is for today have missed this basic principle, GOD DOES NOT CHANGE! There are some who believe that the *offering of the tithe* was just under the Law. However, *tithing* was GOD'S method for giving before, during, and after the Law.

Abraham paid *tithes* to Melchizedek before the Law. **Genesis 14:20**

Tithing was continued under the Law. **Leviticus 27:30**

Jesus taught that men should *tithe.* **Matthew 23:23**

The writer of Hebrews taught that **"men that die here"** might receive *tithes*. This was after the resurrection of Jesus and during this present Church Age. **Hebrews 7:8**

In **Exodus 25** and **Exodus 36**, they brought these *tithes* and *offerings* into God's House to build a Sanctuary. So then the *tithe* is brought to the House of God.

3. The Free-Will Offering

GOD introduced a third financial system that was given to the people after the weeks of harvest were over. It was called a free-will offering. It was not the same thing as the tithe. It was completely different!

"And thou shalt keep the feast of weeks unto the LORD thy God with a tribute of a FREEWILL OFFERING of thine hand, which thou shalt give unto the LORD thy God, according as the LORD thy God hath blessed thee:" Deuteronomy 16:10

Notice the second part of that verse, **"according as the Lord thy God hath blessed thee."** You can give as much as you want to in this offering or as little as you want to. It's your decision.

This is the offering that Jesus refers to in **Luke 6:38**:

"Give, and it shall be given unto you; good measure, pressed down, and shaken together, and running over, shall men give into your bosom. For with the same measure that ye mete withal it shall be measured to you again."

One preacher said, God uses the same scoop that you do. The size of our next financial harvest is determined by the size of the free-will offering that we give today.

Then I read in the Scripture where God's people were lacking and were not blessed. They were living under a financial curse. This story is found in **Malachi 3**. God spoke to the nation of Israel through his prophet Malachi. Israel's finances were cursed and the covenant of blessing was not working for them.

Here was God's Challenge:

"For I am the Lord, I change not; therefore, ye sons of Jacob are not consumed. **Even from the days of your fathers ye are gone away from mine ordinances, and have not kept them. Return unto me, and I will return unto you, saith the LORD of Hosts. But ye said, Wherein shall we return?" Malachi 3:6,7**

They didn't even know where they were missing it. You know what I have learned in preaching over the years? I can preach and there are folks who come, I mean good folks, wonderful people, precious people; but they don't realize there might be an area in their life where they're missing it. That is why we need the preaching of the Word.

"Will a man rob God? Yet ye have robbed me. But ye say, Wherein have we robbed thee? IN TITHES AND OFFERINGS." Malachi 3:8

They didn't even know where they were stealing from God. Notice, God doesn't allow ignorance to be an excuse. He says come on back to the right thing. *Where have we robbed you?* He says, in *tithes*, that's **Leviticus 27:30,32** and *offerings,* that's the *free-will offering* of **Deuteronomy 16:10.**

PAYING TITHES WAS NOT ENOUGH TO REMOVE THE CURSE OFF OF THEIR FINANCES.

There were two distinct financial systems mentioned in **Malachi 3:8;** *Tithes and offerings.* Because they were not practicing God's Financial Systems, they were not being blessed.

You cannot break the spirit of debt in your life until you begin to faithfully use God's Financial Systems. It is time to break the spirit of debt and the demonic wall of containment off our money in Jesus Name!

"Bring ye all the tithes into the storehouse, that there may be meat in mine house, and prove me now herewith, saith the

LORD of hosts, if I will not open you the windows of heaven, and pour you out a blessing, that there shall not be room enough to receive it.

And I will rebuke the devourer for your sakes, and he shall not destroy the fruits of your ground; neither shall your vine cast her fruit before the time in the field, saith the LORD of hosts." Malachi 3:10-11

A Blind Woman Receives Her Sight

When I was working with Brother Schambach, he told me the story of how a woman that was blind received her sight when she promised God that she would do something.

Brother Schambach was working with Evangelist A.A. Allen in the early days of his ministry. He told me that he learned many great lessons in Brother Allen's meetings.

A.A. Allen had put up his Gospel tent in one of the great cities of America. Night after night, the people came to hear the Word of God and to be healed. There was one woman who was blind that came through the prayer line every night. After several nights, Brother Allen stopped her and said to her, *"Sister, the Lord shows me that there is something that you are not doing and it is hindering your healing."*

The woman walked down the ramp and when she got to the bottom she bowed her head and said, *"Alright Lord, I'll pay my tithes!"* When she said that her blind eyes came open!

Brother Schambach told me he said, *"Me too Lord!"* I laughed because the way he related the story to me was funny, but the lesson is powerful. When we obey God in paying our tithes and giving offerings, THE BLESSING is not hindered.

What if this were the only thing that was keeping you from operating in THE BLESSING? The Bible says that, **"Behold, to obey it is better than sacrifice and to hearken than the fat of rams." 1 Samuel 15:22**

Saul had disobeyed God's Instruction. He was to destroy everything that Amalek had. Yet when Saul saw what the Amalekites had, he kept the best of the sheep, oxen, fatlings (cows), lambs, and all of the possessions that were good. He disobeyed God.

Because Saul rejected God's Word and disobeyed the Lord, then he was rejected that day as being the king. Our position in life is determined by our obedience. Obedience is the key to prosperity.

Attitude determines altitude. Man looks on the outward, but God looks on the heart. Poverty and lack are a direct result of rejecting the instructions that are contained in the Word of God.

I've made up my mind I'm going to have everything God has for me!

CHAPTER EIGHT
HOW TO LIVE IN THE BLESSING AND ENJOY LIFE

One of my favorite scriptures is found in **Jeremiah 29:11 NIV**

"For I know the PLANS I have for you, declares the Lord, PLANS to prosper you and not to harm you, PLANS to give you hope and a future."

There are three things that God has planned for YOUR life:

PLANS to prosper YOU.

PLANS to give YOU hope.

PLANS to give YOU a future.

God has got YOU covered! The Bible is very plain about the fact that the Lord wants His children to succeed in everything that we do. YOU are created by God to be successful and enjoy a good life.

"And also that every man should eat and drink, and ENJOY THE GOOD of all his labour, it is the gift of God." Ecclesiastes 3:13

God wants YOU and YOUR FAMILY to enjoy a GOOD LIFE!

"Behold that which I have seen: it is good and comely for one to eat and to drink, and to enjoy the GOOD of all his labour that he taketh under the sun ALL THE DAYS OF HIS LIFE, which God giveth him: for it is his portion." Ecclesiastes 5:18

Jesus taught that He came to undo the force of evil that was trying to keep us from enjoying the good life. He told His followers:

"The thief cometh not, but for to steal, and to kill, and to destroy: I am come that they might have life, and that they might have it more ABUNDANTLY." John 10:10

The Living Bible paraphrases it this way; **"MY PURPOSE is to give life in all its fullness."**

The *NIV* records this verse as, **"I have come that they may have life, and have it to the FULL."**

The Lord wants you to have a good life. His plan and purpose is that you might live your life full of blessing and abundance. Jesus wants you to be filled with joy as a testimony of God's faithfulness in a day when many are filled with fear. His plan is that you might prosper and have an abundant supply. God does not want you to fail.

Jesus spoke to Peter about his future. He told him that the devil would like to destroy him and keep him from the life that He had for him. Jesus said, **"But I have prayed for thee, that thy faith FAIL NOT:"** Luke 22:32

The plan that God has for your life produces hope! Don't give up! Never quit! God's Word declares that the best is yet to come! There is hope in Jesus Christ!

I believe that the there is a key to seeing our life's plan succeed.

I base this upon the Scripture. It is very simple. When you and I seek to bring God's Plan to pass then He will cause our life's plan to succeed as well. What is God's Plan? God wants men and women everywhere to be saved!

"The Lord is not slack concerning his promise, as some men count slackness; but is longsuffering to us-ward, NOT WILLING THAT ANY SHOULD PERISH, but that all should come to REPENTANCE."

2 Peter 3:9

Our prosperity comes from our understanding that God's Priority is that men and women need to be saved. I believe that every day He releases the amount of money that is needed to bring this to pass. There is always *"more than enough"* for His Work and your good life!

What I Learned From Mark Buntain When I Went to India

As I have traveled all over the world in crusades, it seems to me that people are basically the same. Fathers want to provide for their families. Mothers want to have a good home. Children dream their dreams of the future. God wants the families of the world to be blessed. Yet, it is obvious that many nations of the world are suffering.

I went to India when I was 26 years old. The great missionary Mark Buntain had opened the doors for me to minister for him in Calcutta. How inadequate my ministry was. Yet, looking back there was something that the Lord wanted me to learn.

Brother Buntain was a man of prayer. He seemed to draw compassion from Christ in those early morning prayer vigils. One morning, when we had finished praying, he told me that it was his birthday. I asked him if I could give him a gift. He told me, *"Come,*

I'll show you what I want."

We drove to a big field. There were multiplied thousands of women and children standing in long lines as far as you could see. Brother Buntain told me that many had walked all night to stand in line to get a cup of soup and a chapatti (bread). Then he said they would turn around and walk home to share it with their families.

"Do you have money for these souls?" Brother Buntain asked me. I had flown from Bombay to Calcutta on Air India. Mother Theresa sat in front of me she was returning from the United States where she had been raising money for her work. Mark Buntain needed money for his work. There it was friend, the truth that I traveled around the globe to find. MY MONEY COULD HELP WIN SOULS TO CHRIST!

Obeying The Great Commission

Did you know that God is happy and takes extreme delight when His servants prosper?

"Let them shout for joy, and be glad, that favour my RIGHTEOUS CAUSE: yea, let them say continually, Let the LORD be magnified, which hath pleasure in THE PROSPERITY OF HIS SERVANT." Psalm 35:27

Why does God want you to have an abundance of money? It is because He wants you to be able to *"favor"* His righteous cause with your prosperity. We can use our money for the winning of souls.

There are two verses of Scripture that prove to me why the Lord will bless His children financially.

"And he said unto them, GO ye into all the world, and preach the gospel to every creature. He that believeth and is baptized

shall be saved; but he that believeth not shall be damned." Mark 16:15,16

"And HOW shall they preach, except they be sent? as it is written, How beautiful are the feet of them that preach the gospel of peace, and bring glad tidings of good things!" Romans 10:15

The "HOW" determines the "GO"!

God blesses us to be a blessing! This to me is one of the main reasons why I believe God wants to prosper His children. The GOSPEL must be preached! It takes money to send out the preacher and the message of ETERNAL LIFE.

If Jesus does not want us to have the money, then He does not want the GOSPEL to be preached!

The Great Commission must be obeyed! When we work to fulfill this command of Christ, then we must expect to receive material possessions in this life.

"And Jesus answered and said, Verily I say unto you, There is no man that hath left house, or brethren, or sisters, or father, or mother, or wife, or children, or lands, FOR MY SAKE and THE GOSPEL'S,

But HE SHALL RECEIVE AN HUNDREDFOLD NOW IN THIS TIME, . . ." Mark 10:29,30

Jonah's Disobedience

God wanted to save 120,000 souls in Nineveh, but it displeased Jonah and made him mad. God wanted to use him to preach repentance to Nineveh. Jonah decided he would not do it and he disobeyed God.

He used his money to go on a cruise. The Bible records these interesting words, **"He paid the fare thereof." Jonah 1:3** It will always cost us to go our own way. God is only responsible to provide for what He tells us to do.

Jonah found himself cast overboard and in the belly of a great fish, because of his disobedience. He could have used his money to fulfill his "commission" from God to preach in Nineveh, but instead, he used it for his own selfish desires.

Jonah had used his money wrongly. He prayed and promised the Lord that he would use his money to fulfill his promise.

"But I will sacrifice unto thee with the voice of thanksgiving; I will PAY that that I have VOWED. Salvation is of the LORD." Jonah 2:9

When Jonah got his thinking right about his money, then God gave him a second chance. The Lord caused Jonah to be vomited upon dry land. Jonah obeyed god and Nineveh repented. When it looks like there is no way out, God can make a way. You can move God with your offering.

"VOW, and PAY unto the LORD your God: let all that be round about him bring presents unto him that ought to be feared. He shall cut off the spirit of princes: he is terrible to the kings of the earth." Psalm 76:11-12

The key to prosperity is obedience! Obedience to God's Word and to His Will. Always give God the glory for your blessings and remember that:

". . .for it is he that giveth thee POWER TO GET WEALTH, that he may ESTABLISH HIS COVENANT which he sware unto thy fathers, as it is this day. Deuteronomy 8:18

CHAPTER NINE
HOW GOD TAKES WHAT YOU HAVE AND TURNS IT INTO WHAT YOU NEED

The first miracle of Jesus was a miracle of provision. The Lord cares about our needs. His Word assures us that,

"**For the LORD God is a sun and shield: the LORD will give grace and glory: NO GOOD THING WILL HE WITHHOLD from them that walk uprightly." Psalm 84:11**

When we learn how God operates and works to provide, then we can access that same power so that we may receive miracles of provision as well. What God does for one He will do for everyone. God has a miracle of provision for you!

The first miracle of Jesus is recorded in **John 2**. Jesus and His disciples were invited to a marriage in Cana of Galilee. The mother of Jesus was there and when Jesus arrived she told Him that they had run out of wine.

"**Jesus saith unto her, Woman, what have I to do with thee? mine hour is not yet come." John 2:4**

I find it interesting that the mother of Jesus answered His question with a bold statement of faith. She said to the servants that were standing nearby,

"Whatsoever he saith unto you, DO IT." John 2:5

Faith is an action based upon a belief supported by a confession. Remember this progression. The ABC's of Faith. A is action, B is belief, and C is confession. She said, *"Whatsoever he saith, do it."* She believed that Jesus could do something about what was lacking.

You and I are bombarded with questions about our financial future. *What phase of the economic challenge are we in? Is the financial crisis going to get worse? What should I do about my future?*

There are some people who see lack and worry. The mother of Jesus saw lack and knew that Jesus could fix the problem. There is nothing that can happen to you that Jesus can't do something about it!

What they needed was wine, what they had was water. Here we see this principle in action. Jesus told them to **"Fill the waterpots with water." John 2:7**

God takes what you have and turns it into what you need. The Anointing for provision was released when the servants obeyed the Word of God. Miracles flow out of God's Word.

"So then faith cometh by hearing, and hearing by the Word of God." Romans 10:17

Jesus told them to fill up the water pots and when they did what Jesus said then the miracle was released. You and I must find a word in the Scripture that covers our need and stand on it until the provision comes.

"And HE SAITH unto them, DRAW out now, and BEAR to the governor of the feast. And they bare it.

When the ruler of the feast had tasted the water that was made wine, and knew not whence it was: (but the servants which drew the water knew;) the governor of the feast called the bridegroom,

And saith unto him, Every man at the beginning doth set forth good wine; and when men have well drunk, then that which is worse: BUT THOU HAST KEPT THE GOOD WINE UNTIL NOW." John 2:8-10

When Mary, mother of Jesus, said *"Whatsoever he saith unto you do it."* then I think that we can examine what Jesus said before the water became wine to help us understand how supernatural provision is released for me and you.

The first word Jesus spoke was, **"FILL."** vs. 7

He chose to use empty waterpots. Their condition was not a hindrance, but merely what Jesus would use to meet the need. *They had empty water pots and He would take what they had and turn it into what they needed.*

The second word Jesus spoke was, **"DRAW."** vs. 8

Here is where the servants cooperated with the miracle of provision. God performs miracles through men and women who believe His Word. The book of **Acts** tells us how God worked through the natural efforts of the Apostles.

"And by the HANDS of the apostles were many SIGNS AND WONDERS wrought among the people;" Acts 5:12

God works miracles through the lives of those who will believe Him.

When the servants came to the governor of the feast, he said,

"Every man at the beginning doth set forth good wine; and when men have well drunk, then that which is worse: but THOU HAST KEPT THE GOOD WINE UNTIL NOW." John 2:10

Your best is yet to come. Your future is secure when you place what you have into the Master's Hands. God has planned a great life for you. *Any lack that you may experience does not define who you are and what God will do for you!*

A Woman Becomes An Oil Tycoon Overnight

"Now there cried a certain woman of the wives of the sons of the prophets unto Elisha, saying, Thy servant my husband is dead; and thou knowest that thy servant did fear the Lord: and the creditor is come to take unto him my two sons to be bondmen.

And Elisha said unto her, What shall I do for thee? tell me, WHAT HAST THOU IN THE HOUSE? And she said, Thine handmaid hath not any thing in the house, SAVE A POT OF OIL." 2 Kings 4:1, 2

Once again, we see this principle repeated in this story. GOD TAKES WHAT YOU HAVE AND TURNS IT INTO WHAT YOU NEED. The prophet asked her what she had in the house. Her answer was that she didn't really have anything. . .wait a minute, there is a pot of oil.

She saw herself with nothing. The prophet wanted her to take inventory of her possessions. Her debt seemed bigger than her assets. There are a lot of people in this position today. *As long as we magnify the problem then we cannot clearly see the answer.*

"Believe in the Lord your God, so shall ye be established; believe his prophets, so shall ye prosper." 2 Chronicles 20:20

Elisha the prophet was speaking into the woman's life so that she could be secure and prosperous as a family. The word *"established"* in this scripture is also translated *"kept safe."* The marginal rendering in my Bible refers to **Isaiah 7:9** where the phrase is recorded **"If you will not believe, surely you shall not be established." [made secure]**

Our believing determines our receiving. If you don't believe God's Word you can't receive from God's Word.

Elisha was a prophet of God. The woman needed a miracle. He got her to use what she had so that she could have what she needed. She said, *"I have a pot of oil."* Then, he gave her the instructions (a Word from God) that would produce a supernatural supply. Literally, she became an oil tycoon overnight!

Her sons gathered the pots from the neighbors. She began to pour out until the last vessel was full. Then the oil stopped. *Your expectation determines the size of your blessing.*

THE BLESSING is as big as you want it to be. There is no limit to God's Provision. Take a step of faith and learn to give to the Lord's Work. God will bless you

Years ago, my wife and I traveled as evangelists without a home or an apartment. We did this for 10 years. If we did not have meetings we would stay with our parents. I did not have the understanding of THE BLESSING as I do now.

It was January and we were in Virginia at my parents home. Dad and Mom had gone to California to preach and were gone for the month. All my Dad asked me to do was keep the house heated and buy kerosene for the heaters. One night, my wife said, *"This is the last of the food."* She had taken the last of the hamburger and made a little meatloaf with Velveeta cheese inside. That meatloaf shrunk when she cooked it. When she put it on the table that was it, the last of the food.

I didn't have money for kerosene, my car payment, my insurance payment, or any more food. I bowed my head to pray and I began to thank the Lord for what we had. We needed more than this, but somehow I understood to thank Him for what I had. When I began to pray the anointing came on me and I began to praise God for His faithfulness.

Suddenly, I knew that my friend would call me and give me $1,000. The phone rang while I was praising God. I got up from the table and answered it, *"Hello Joe!"*

"How did you know it was me?" We did not have Caller ID in those days. I had Holy Ghost ID! *"The Lord told me you would call and that you had a check for me."* I didn't even give him a chance to talk. I asked him, *"Where do you want to meet? I need the check right now."*

He said, *"Cathy must have told you."* That was his wife and he thought she had let me know what he was going to do. When I told him that the check was for $1,000 he was surprised because he knew he had not told his wife how much it was. I told him, *"I'll meet you down the street at Dominion Bank."* I hung up the phone and ran out the door. When he showed up in the parking lot I grabbed the check and thanked him and ran to the bank to make the deposit before the bank closed. Then, I went over to the Food Lion grocery store and grabbed two carts. I went straight to the meat department first. I put t-bone steaks in the cart, whole chickens, a side of ham, and bacon.

Then I went over to the produce department and loaded up on lettuce, tomatoes, carrots, onions, and green beans. I put a whole bag of potatoes in the cart. I shopped until we had all the food we would need for the rest of the month.

Next, I went to the gas station, filled up my car, and bought kerosene for the heaters at the house. When I got home I told my wife to put the meatloaf in the refrigerator and we fixed a feast!

I had $100 for my tithes, $169 for my car payment, I had $32 for my insurance, enough money to heat the house and buy food for the month. You know what was an even greater blessing? I had hundreds of dollars left to live on. THE BLESSING WORKS!!

A Sore That Needs To Be Healed

"There is a SORE EVIL which I have seen under the sun, namely, RICHES KEPT for the owners thereof to their hurt." **Ecclesiastes 5:13**

It is increasingly evident that this worldly attitude has crept into the Church. Many Christians have held back their monies that could have been used for the preaching of the Gospel.

It is this sin of selfishness that must be repented of. It is not a sin to prosper and it is God's Will that you do prosper. However, there is a purpose for prosperity. God revealed this truth to Moses in His covenant of blessing.

"But thou shalt remember the LORD thy God: for it is he that giveth thee power to get wealth, that he may ESTABLISH HIS COVENANT which he sware unto thy fathers, as it is this day." **Deuteronomy 8:18**

There is a decision that every believer must make when God begins to prosper him. It can be summed up in these words. *Riches kept or riches spent.* Remember, the Bible teaches this paradox. What you keep you lose and what you sow comes back to you.

"There is that scattereth, and yet increaseth; and there is that

withholdeth MORE THAN IS MEET, but it tendeth to poverty." Proverbs 11:24

When you keep more than you should, by that I mean you hold on to what the Lord has spoken to you to give, then it will eventually bring **"hurt"** and **"poverty"** to you. This is a biblical and a thoroughly scriptural principle. We are to be givers and not hoarders.

God wants you to turn it loose! We are to sow our blessings that we might bless others. This unselfish spirit is the Spirit of Christ.

When Jesus challenged the rich young ruler to give of his wealth to the poor, he refused to do so and the Bible says, **"he went away SORROWFUL: for he had great possessions." Matthew 19:22**

Notice, the **"riches kept"** brought him **"hurt"** and *sorrow*. He left in a sad condition. If he had given to the poor as Jesus had instructed him, it would have been returned to him according to God's Word!

"He that hath pity upon the poor lendeth unto the LORD; and that which he hath given will he pay him again." Proverbs 19:17

Don't be too hard on this rich young ruler. Many of us have refused to give of our monies to help the poor and the lost of this world. *Is it because we have forgotten that riches spent are better than riches kept?*

God considers your giving as a loan when you help the poor. He has promised to pay it back and He always pays with interest. THE GREATEST INVESTMENT THAT YOU CAN MAKE IS INTO A SOUL-WINNING MINISTRY!

The Purpose of Prosperity

There is a direct connection between God's Plan and Provision. There is a purpose for the prosperity that He releases to you and me. When we get that understanding then our prosperity will increase.

There is a priority to our prosperity. Jesus taught on this priority in His Sermon on the Mount.

"But seek ye first the kingdom of God, and his righteousness; and all these things shall be added unto you." Matthew 6:33

God does not mind you being blessed. God wants you to have houses and lands. He wants you to be clothed. He desires to give His children the desires of their heart. However, these things are added to our life as we seek God's purpose and plan for His Kingdom.

God's Covenant Blessing is very simple to understand. When you and I work to establish His great Kingdom on the earth; He releases the wealth to us for this purpose. The question then is what must we do to accomplish this?

What was it that Jesus told His disciples to do?

The Unfulfilled Commission

The Great Commission that Jesus gave to us that are His disciples is found in the Gospels.

"Go ye therefore, and teach all nations, baptizing them in the name of the Father, and of the Son, and of the Holy Ghost:

Teaching them to observe all things whatsoever I have commanded you: and, lo, I am with you alway, even unto the

end of the world. Amen." Matthew 28:19-20

There was one single purpose in Christ's coming to earth. That single purpose was left to the Church to accomplish. It is our number one job. What was the purpose in Christ's coming?

"For this purpose the Son of God was manifested, that he might destroy the works of the devil". 1 John 3:8

The assignment that Jesus gave the disciples was to preach the Gospel with signs following to the entire world. Mark 16:19, 20 It is this message followed by signs and wonders and miracles that destroys the works of the devil!

"And this gospel of the kingdom shall be preached in all the world for a WITNESS unto all nations; and then shall the end come". Matthew 24:14

The word **"witness"** translates, *"evidence."* The Gospel must be preached with evidence. There are two things that are immediately understood. (1) The Gospel is to be preached to the whole world. (2) It is to be confirmed by God with signs and wonders.

We know what we must do to fulfill the Great Commission. It will take all of our prayers that we can pray. It will take all of the money that we can give. It will take all of the sacrifice that we can make. Remember, it cost Jesus His life! John Wesley, the founder of Methodism, wrote:

> DO ALL the GOOD you can
> By ALL the Means you can
> By ALL the Ways you can
> In ALL the Places you can
> In ALL the Times you can
> To ALL the people you can
> As long as YOU ever can!